01209 722146

Duchy College Rosewarne
Learning Centre

This resource is to be returned on or before the last date stamped below. To renew items please contact the Centre

Three Week Loan

2 1 APR 2017		

The World's Deadliest

The Deadliest Bugs

on Earth

by Erika Shores

www.raintreepublishers.co.uk
Visit our website to find out
more information about
Raintree books.

To order:
☏ Phone 0845 6044371
🖹 Fax +44 (0) 1865 312263
✉ Email myorders@raintreepublishers.co.uk

Customers from outside the UK please telephone +44 1865 312262

Raintree is an imprint of Capstone Global
Library Limited, a company incorporated
in England and Wales having its registered
office at 7 Pilgrim Street, London,
EC4V 6LB – Registered company number:
6695582

Text © Capstone Press 2010
First published in hardback in the United
Kingdom by Capstone Global Library in 2011
The moral rights of the proprietor have
been asserted.

Edited by Abby Czeskleba
Designed by Matt Bruning
Media research by Svetlana Zhurkin
Production by Laura Manthe
Originated by Capstone Global Library Ltd
Printed and bound in China by South China
Printing Company Ltd

ISBN 978 1 406 21829 9
14 13 12 11 10
10 9 8 7 6 5 4 3 2 1

**British Library Cataloguing in Publication
Data**
Shores, Erika L.
The deadliest bugs on Earth. -- (The world's
deadliest)
595.7'165-dc22
A full catalogue record for this book is available
from the British Library.

Acknowledgements
We would like to thank the following for
permission to reproduce photographs:
Alamy pp. **7** (Phototake/Scott Camazine),
27 (David Haynes); CDC pp. **11**, **29** (James
Gathany); Corbis pp. **9** (Martin Harvey), **22**
(Gallo Images/Anthony Bannister); Getty
Images p. **21** (Ian Waldie); iStockphoto
p. **5** (Mark Kostich); Peter Arnold pp. **13**
(Bios/Alain Beignet), **25** (David Scharf);
Photolibrary pp. **16** (John Brown), **19** (Oxford
Scientific/Brian Kenney); Photo Researchers
p. **15** (Scott Camazine).

Cover photographs reproduced with kind
permission of Alamy (David Haynes) - spider;
Shutterstock (Alexander Potapov) - web;
Brandon Blinkenberg - wasp.

Disclaimer
All the Internet addresses (URLs) given in this
book were valid at the time of going to press.
However, due to the dynamic nature of the
Internet, some addresses may have changed,
or sites may have changed or ceased to exist
since publication. While the author and
publisher regret any inconvenience this may
cause readers, no responsibility for any such
changes can be accepted by either the author
or the publisher.

CONTENTS

Some words are printed in bold, **like this**. You can find out what they mean on page 30. You can also look in the box at the bottom of the page where they first appear.

MANY-LEGGED KILLERS

Creeping, crawling, buzzing bugs can be more than garden pests. Some minibeasts have deadly **venom** in their bites or stings that can kill.

venom poisonous liquid made by some minibeasts

SLIGHTLY
DANGEROUS

DANGER
Meter

HIDDEN
DANGER

The brown recluse spider lives in North America. It hides inside and outside people's homes. The **venom** in its bite can kill **tissue**. A bite can leave a deep hole in a person's skin.

tissue soft material that animals and plants are made of

DEADLY SOLDIERS

Army ants live in huge groups. Up to 100,000 army ants can march on land. Stay out of their way. Bites from army ants hurt. They can be deadly to people who have **allergic reactions**.

allergic reaction unpleasant reaction such as a rash, breathing problem, or sneezing

A SCARY SPIDER

The black widow is North America's most **venomous** spider. This spider's bite releases **venom**. People can have muscle pains and problems breathing from a black widow's bite.

DEADLY *FACT*

Female black widow spiders weigh 30 times more than males.

venomous having or making a poison called venom

VERY DANGEROUS

STEALING YOUR FOOD

Locusts fly in giant **swarms**. They travel hundreds of kilometres each day. Locusts chew up and destroy crops. Without crops, people die because there is not enough food to eat.

swarm group of insects that gather and move in large numbers

DEADLY FACT

Some swarms have about
100 million locusts.

BEWARE THE STING

Asian giant hornets are the world's largest hornets. They sting with sharp jabs. **Allergic reactions** to stings kill about 50 people a year.

DEADLY FACT

An Asian giant hornet's stinger is more than 6 millimetres long.

RUN AWAY

Africanized honeybees are also called killer bees. If bothered, these bees attack in deadly **swarms**. Thousands of stings from angry bees can kill.

DEADLY *FACT*

Do not dive into water to escape killer bees. They will be waiting for you when you come up to breathe.

READY TO STING

In Africa, fat-tailed scorpions live in the cracks of walls. Fat-tailed scorpions attack with their sharp stingers. Stings from these scorpions kill more than 35 people every year.

DEADLY FACT

There are about 1,500 species of scorpions. Only 25 have deadly **venom**.

19

EXTREMELY DANGEROUS

DANGER Meter

BIG FANGS

A Sydney funnel-web spider's fangs are the size of a cat's claws. The spider's fangs sink into their **prey** and release **venom**. A person can die within one hour of being bitten.

prey animal hunted by another animal for food

DEADLY FACT

Male funnel-web spiders are six times more **venomous** than females.

YOU'RE GETTING SLEEPY

The tsetse fly's bite carries an illness called sleeping sickness. People bitten by a tsetse fly can suffer fevers and headaches. The illness can be deadly if people do not see a doctor.

DEADLY FACT

In Africa, 25,000 people catch sleeping sickness each year.

PUCKER UP

Kissing bugs are found in South America. They get their name because they bite near people's mouths. The bite can give people Chagas' disease. The disease causes fevers, tiredness, and sometimes death.

DEADLY FACT

Kissing bugs usually bite at night when people are sleeping.

25

THAT REALLY HURTS

In Brazil, people fear banana spiders. These spiders are one of the world's most **venomous** spiders. A painful bite causes sweating, heart problems, and even death.

TINY KILLERS

Malaria is a disease spread by mosquitoes, which kills a lot of people in Africa. More than 1 million people die every year from malaria. Minibeasts are more than just pests. And they do not have to be big to be dangerous.

malaria serious disease that causes high fever, chills, and sometimes death

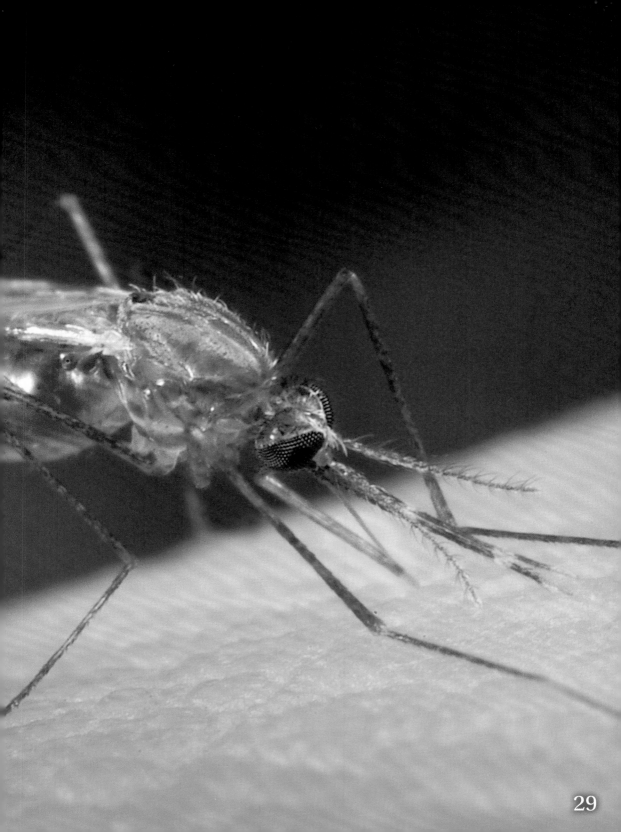

GLOSSARY

allergic reaction unpleasant reaction such as a rash, breathing problem, or sneezing

malaria serious disease that causes high fever, chills, and sometimes death

prey animal hunted by another animal for food

swarm group of insects that gather and move in large numbers

tissue soft material that animals and plants are made of

venom poisonous liquid made by some minibeasts

venomous having or making a poison called venom

FIND OUT MORE

Books

Disgusting Body Facts: Itches and Scratches, Angela Royston (Raintree, 2010)

Disgusting Body Facts: Mites and Bites, Angela Royston (Raintree, 2010)

Extreme! Body Bugs: The Uninvited Guests on Your Body, Trevor Day (A&C Black, 2009)

Websites

http://www.bugsandweeds.co.uk/index.html
Find out about some British minibeasts.

http://www.malariahotspots.co.uk/kids.html
This site has lots of useful information and interesting facts about malaria.

INDEX